TRANSFORM

How To Live The Perfect Life

MARTY HALE

STRAIGHT
TRUTH PRESS

WHAT IS THE PERFECT LIFE?

Ask 1000 people and you'll get 1000 different answers but their would be common threads. Most would say it includes; success and significance. Freedom and Fulfillment, a life well-lived. A life of meaning, purpose, love & laughter, wonder and adventure. Something worth living for and maybe even something worth dying for. To make a difference in the world.

While we might not know exactly what the perfect life is; the Bible says; If you want the perfect life; "Do not be conformed to this world, but be transformed by the renewing of your mind so that you may live the perfect life."

– Romans 12:1-2

THE WHEEL OF LIFE

To balance your most important lifetime goals, think of your life as a wheel with many different spokes. To have a balanced life, each spoke needs your attention. Balance the wheel of your life. Set five-year goals in these (and other) areas.

On a scale of 1 to 7, where 1 means "not at all satisfied with my life" and 7 means "completely satisfied,: the people on "Forbes" magazine's list of the 400 richest Americans average 5.8 - the same as the Inuit people in Greenland and the cattle-herding Masai of Kenya, who live in dung huts with no electricity or nunning water. *(From " Money Really Doesn't Buy Happiness" Whitley Strieber)*

RELATIONSHIP

HE

SPIRITUAL

ROMANCE

LI

RECREATION

TRAVEL

EDUCATION

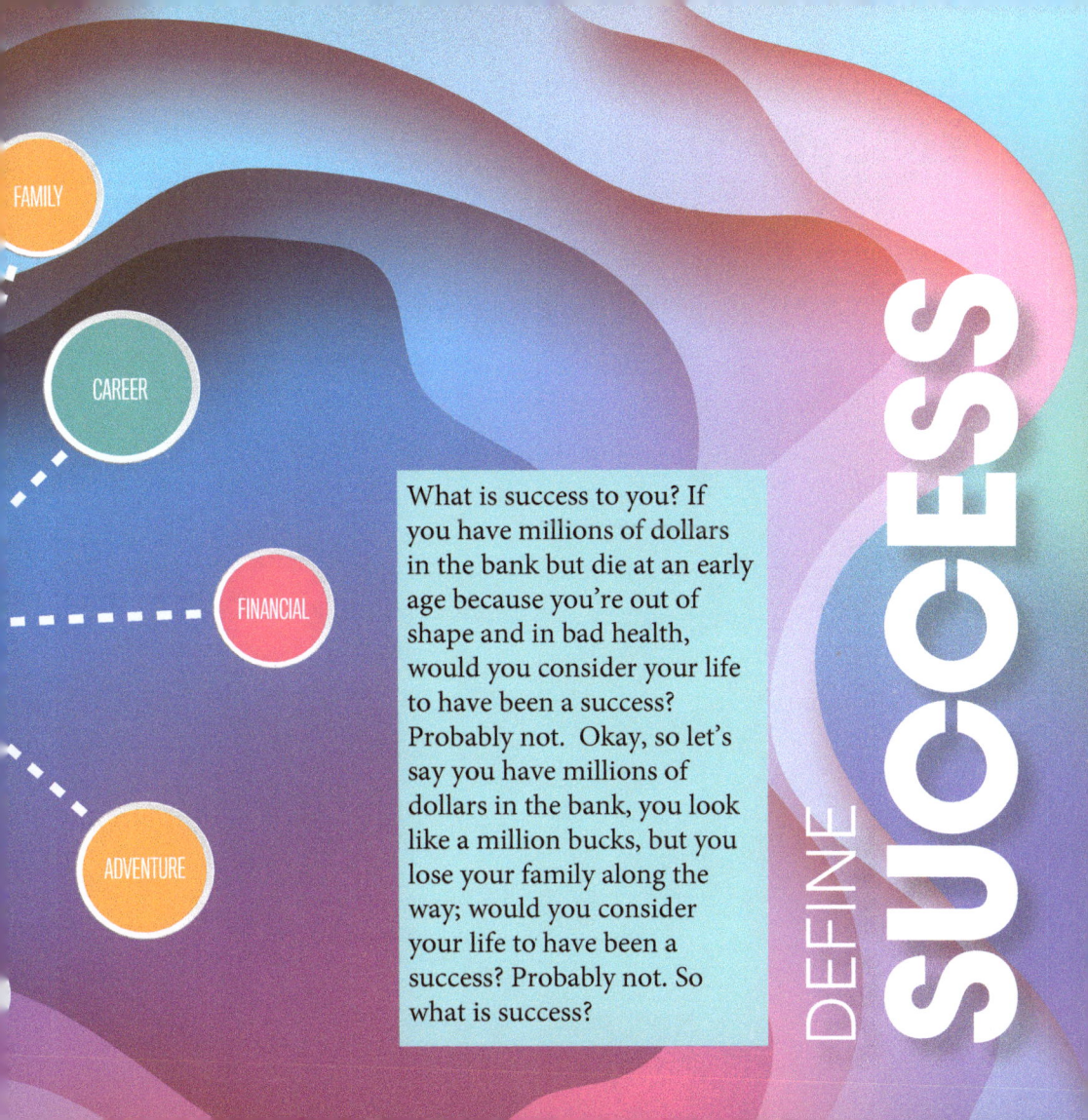

FAMILY

CAREER

FINANCIAL

ADVENTURE

DEFINE SUCCESS

What is success to you? If you have millions of dollars in the bank but die at an early age because you're out of shape and in bad health, would you consider your life to have been a success? Probably not. Okay, so let's say you have millions of dollars in the bank, you look like a million bucks, but you lose your family along the way; would you consider your life to have been a success? Probably not. So what is success?

THE CYCLE OF
TRANSFO

RMATION

IF YOU WANT TO TRANSFORM AND RE-INVENT YOUR FUTURE IT STARTS HERE, WITH THE TRUTH!

The Cycle of Transformation

One's **DESIRE** determines everything. It determines your **EPISTEMOLOGY**; how you know what you know, where you get your info. Which determines your **METAPHYSICS**; your understanding of reality, what's real versus what appears to be real. Which determines your **ANTHROPOLOGY**; your view of you and the world around you. Your self image, identity and how you see others.

If you desire anything more than absolute **TRUTH**, it's impossible to discover, much less live your purpose and reach your full potential. Your philosophy must be based on truth or all is meaningless. Your decisions will be based on illusions which appear to be reality. The most important decisions you'll make in life will be based on false information. Now you wouldn't want that would you? No...impossible to live the perfect life.

ALLOW ME TO EXPLAIN:

My senior year in high school my heart was broken by my girlfriend who cheated on me. She happened to wear a very popular perfume. For the next few years every time I'd meet an attractive woman, if they wore that particular perfume I'd run as fast as I could to get away from them. Why? Because I desired an attractive woman more than I desired the truth. You see my desire for an attractive girl was causing me to get my information **(epistemology)** from my human-lived experience (a broken heart) which caused an illusion (they will cheat on me too) to become my understanding of reality

(metaphysics) and therefore my view of the new girl **(anthropology)** was completely wrong and therefore I'd make a decision based on wrong information resulting in failure after failure.

We do this in every aspect of life; when we **Desire** to lose weight more than the truth, we get our info from whatever diet gimmick is hot, rather than the simple truth of eating healthy and exercise.

We often fail financially, spiritually, socially, in relationships, and so many ways because we Desire "things & thoughts" more than **TRUTH**.

Establish a foundation for absolute truth...as being the Bible versus human lived experience.

TAKE THE CHALLENGE

TRANSFORM

Four of the most important questions for man kind:

What do I desire most?

How do I know what I know, where do I get my info?

What's my understanding of reality?
What's real and what only appears to be, but isn't?

What is my personal identity, my self image, who am I?

To make a difference is not a matter of accident, a matter of casual occurrence of the tides. People choose to make a difference.
– Maya Angelou

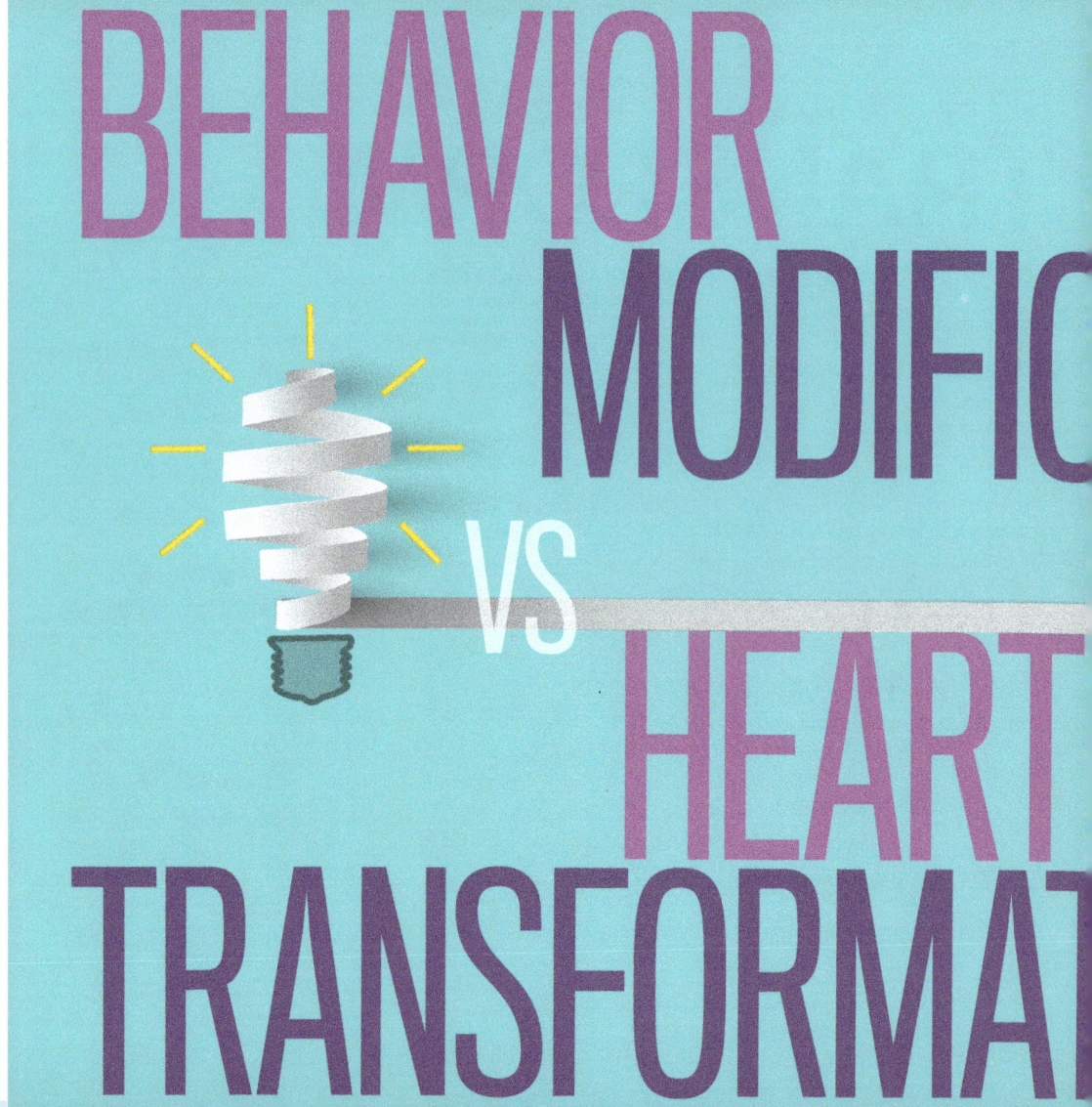

BEHAVIOR MODIFIC

VS

HEART TRANSFORMAT

Many believe that change starts on the outside, if they modify their behavior, in other words; do, do, do they will be, be, be.
Example; take a criminal off the street, modify their behavior and they will change. However that is not absolute **TRUTH**. Many return to doing the same exact behavior and even worse when they're released. **Why is that?**

Their **HEART** wasn't **TRANSFORMED.** Real change happens from the inside. One has to become before they do. Much like the butterfly one must dissolve from the **INSIDE** before they can **FLY.**

1. What is wrong about your philosophy?

2. How will you change it?

REINVENTING

What does it mean to dissolve one self?
How? Why?

The Butterfly is a marvelous example of transformation. An egg is laid by a butterfly and hatches into a caterpillar. The caterpillar eats and eats and eats. As soon as it's done eating, they form themselves into a pupa, also known as a chrysalis. Inside the cocoon it becomes a pure liquid without skeletal structure, IT DISSOLVES ITSELF. What happens next is majestical, out emerges a butterfly. It pumps blood into the wings in order to get them working and flapping – then they take flight.

The most amazing aspect to me is that the DNA of the Caterpillar is the exact DNA of the Pupa and the Butterfly. It's the identical living organism throughout the entire process, but very different in capabilities and responsibilities. The Caterpillar crawls, the butterfly flies. The Caterpillar's job is to eat. The Butterflies job is to reproduce.

Both are equally beautiful, but the real beauty lies in the transformation process. The same is true for us. If you're ready to stop crawling and start flying, it all starts here. Today, right now begin reinventing yourself from the INSIDE OUT.

YOURSELF

WHAT IS THE PERFECT LIFE?

There has never been another you. You are a once-in-all-history event. You are new to nature. You are one of a kind; therefore, no one can really predict to what heights you might soar. Even you will not know until you spread your wings. You may not be able to see your undeveloped potential, but it's there—and it is enormous!

THE
TRANSFORM
PROCESS

BELIEVE

ADMIT

CHANGE

DIE

LIVE

It starts with YOUR internal VALUES & BELIEFS:

1. What is the 1 thing I believe and value most in life?

2. What is the most important thing in my life?

3. Am I willing to die for this belief?

4. Who am I?

"Changing your philosophy, changes your life"

- Marty Hale

You are not here by mistake.

Statistically, the probability of any one of us being born exactly as we are in this precise time and place is so unlikely that your very existence verges on the miraculous and should be a continuing source of dazzlement for you.

Odds of bowling a 300 game: **1 in 11,500**

ODDS

Odds of being hit by a lightning: **1 in 56,000**

OF

Odds of getting a royal flush on your first five cards: **1 in 649,740**

YOUR

Odds of being U.S. president: **1 in 10,000,000**

BEING

Odds of winning $340 million jackpot in MegaMillions lottery: **about 1 in 175,000,000**

BORN

Odds of your being born in this particular time, place and circumstance: **about 1 in 400,000,000,000****

THAN WHY ARE YOU HERE?
BORN, ALIVE...?

The human mind is the fastest-working, coolest-running, most compact and efficient computer ever produced in large quantities by unskilled labor.
— Bob Monawad

YOUR AMAZING MIND...

The average human brain weighs about 2 1/2 to 3 pounds. It is made up of about 30 billion cells called neurons. Each neuron is capable of handling approximately one million bits of information. The total number is so large, in fact, that if you sat down and wrote a number one, you would have to follow it with 6.5 million miles of zeros, a number that would stretch from the Earth to the moon and back more than 13 times.

YOUR AMAZING BODY...

Your body has approximately 62,000 miles of capillaries millions of electrical warning signals, railroad and conveyer systems; a fabulous built-in telephone system; and a highly sophisticated audio-visual system.

YOUR AMAZING SOUL...

You are created in the image of God. Who created the world and all that's in it in 7 days. What image does that give you?

_____

_____

Around the world and down through the ages there has never been another you, and there will never be another you. The miracle of your existence is now in your hands. You are here for a purpose. You have something that only **YOU** can give to the world.

WHAT CAN YOU DO?

BELIEVE

A. It starts with you believing that there is a Power inside you that is able to do exceedingly, abundantly, beyond, all that you can ask, think or imagine. Do you believe this?

B. Here's WHY you must: "As a man thinks, so is he." What you think is who you become. If you don't believe in the Power inside YOU, you will be powerless. Napoleon Hill wrote an entire book on the concept: "Think and Grow Rich".

C. The great separator: Faith. Many say they believe, but there is no evidence (production) that they do. It's merely a thought. faith, however; is the evidence of that which cannot be seen… In other words when one really believes there is EVIDENCE (production) of it. Are you convicted of that which you cannot yet see to the point of creating evidence through your production?

YOU ARE CAPABLE OF AMAZING THINGS

Purpose & Mission

"You have brains in your head and feet in your shoes, you can steer yourself and direction you choose. You're on your own and you know what you know, and you are the one who'll decide where to go." - Dr. Seuss

Imagine it's your 80th birthday, who do you want there with you, and what do you want them to say about your life?

_____

_____

_____

My natural talents and gifts are...

_____

_____

_____

Imagine you life as an epic journey with you as the hero of the story, what would the journey be about?

_____

_____

_____

_____

What I really love to do in life?

_____

_____

_____

live your life on purpose.

What do I consider to be my most important future contribution to the most important people in my life?

_____

_____

_____

I perform at my best when...

_____

_____

_____

If I had unlimited time and financial resources and I knew I could not fail, what would I choose to do?

_____

_____

_____

Discover your true mission

The best day of your life is the day on which you decide your life is your own. No one to lean on, rely on or blame. The gift of life is yours, it is an amazing journey, and you alone are responsible for the quality of it. Life is about the choices you make—choose wisely. Start by choosing the two most important "guiding stars" your values and your mission. CHOOSE YOUR VALUES: Values are personal choices you make about what's important to you. Being guided by your highest values brings immense satisfaction and meaning to life.

EXAMPLES OF PERSONAL MISSION STATEMENTS:

Walt Disney: My mission in life is to make people happy.

Eric Schmidt, CEO of Google: My mission is to collect all the world's information and make it accessible to everyone.

Phil Knight, Founder of Nike: My mission is to bring inspiration and innovation to every athlete in the world.

Considering your answers, write your
PERSONAL MISSION STATEMENT

Ask Yourself, "what is my calling, my life's aim? What inspires me the most? What activity or service is my core values urging me to pursue?"

WHAT CAN YOU DO?

ADMIT YOUR FAULTS

A. What have I done or am still doing that causes me internal shame or guilt?

_____

_____

_____

B. What actions or thoughts of mine bother my conscience?

_____

_____

_____

C. What are some of the largest mistakes in life?

_____

_____

D. Who have I hurt in my life and how?

_____

_____

E. What bad habits do I have right now?

_____

_____

_____

CHANGE YOUR MIND AND ACTIONS

A. Will I change my beliefs? Am I convicted of that which I cannot see?

_____

_____

_____

B. What values and beliefs about me do I need to change right now?

_____

_____

_____

C. What beliefs about others do I need to change?

_____

_____

D. How am I going to treat myself and others differently?

_____

_____

If we have never been amazed by the fact that we exist, we are squandering the greatest fact of all.
-Will Durant

DIE TO SELF

A. Will I let go of the guilt, shame, embarrassment?

YES   **NO**

_____
_____
_____

B. What bad habits or choices am I willing to give up and let go of?

_____
_____
_____

C. Who and what will I give priority to over myself?

_____
_____
_____

D. Do I agree that I am no longer in control of my life, but rather truth is?

_____
_____

E. Will I seek absolute truth to make all decisions of my life?

_____
_____

LIVE ON PURPOSE

A. Don't just live with purpose, live ON purpose. Are you ready? Are you committed? Are you convicted?

_____

_____

_____

_____

_____

_____

The best day of **your life** is the day on which you **decide** your life is your own. No one to lean on, rely on or blame. The girt of life is yours, it is an **amazing journey,** and you alone are responsible for the quality of it. Life is about the choices you make—choose wisely. Start by choosing the most important **"guiding star"** — **the absolute truth**. Being guided by your **purpose brings immense satisfaction and meaning to life.**

"This may be the turning point your
grandchildren will tell stories about
years from now: the time you leap over
the abyss to the other side of the Great
Divide and begin your life in earnest.
On the other hand, this moment of truth
may end up being nothing more than
a brief awakening when you glimpse
what's possible on the other side of the
Great Divide, but then tell yourself, "Nah,
that's way too far to jump."
In that case, your grandchildren will
have to be content talking about what
delicious cookies you used to bake of
what your favorite sports team was. it
will all depend on how brave you'll be."
— Rob Brezsny

Dream & Vision

"if you don't design your own life plan, you'll fall into someone else's and guess what they have planned for you, not much."

— Jim Rohn

DESIGNING YOUR LIFE

Can you think of anything that is a reality today or that exist today that was not first designed or planned? Your shoes? Clothes? Car? Computer? Phone? House?

You get the point; Probably not. Therefore If nothing exists that was not first designed the opposite is also true; if not designed, it' impossible to exist. So regardless of how big or cool your dreams or vision are, if they are no designed or planned th are mere fantasies and impossible to exist.

Consider all the things we plan and design; weddings, vacations, meals, diets, houses. W do we plan weddings? Because we want them to go off without a hitch

We want them to be perfect. What we've dreamed of. What we've envisioned.

What happens when you go to the grocery store without a list? Do you end up getting everything you don't need and forgetting everything you do? Ever taken a long road trip without first mapping out your journey or destination? What happened? You probably ended up taking much longer and even getting lost. What would happen if you built a house without a plan, a blueprint? Just the site of The first storm and it falls apart. If we can't go to the grocery store without a list, take a trip without a map, or build a house without a blueprint, why would anyone go through life without a plan?!

According to Dave Kohl, professor emeritus at Virginia Tech., people who regularly write down their goals earn nine times as much over their lifetimes as the people who don't, and yet 80% of Americans say they don't have goals.

However, setting goals in only one of two areas of life is like rowing a boat with only one oar — you go round and round in only one direction. If you use all your creativity in just one area of your life, you are destined to be one-dimensional in others. (What's the use of being a multi-millionaire if you end up with a broken family or die at an early age?)

Review your Wheel of Life and list your most important dreams below in each area. Include a target date and cost to each one.

"YOUR IMAGINATION IS THE PREVIEW TO LIFE'S COMING ATTRACTIONS."
—ALBERT EINSTEIN

BE SPECIFIC!

When you walk into a restaurant, you don't just say, "Bring me some food." Instead, you're very specific—you pick exactly what you want from the menu.

Do the same for your life. Don't just say, "my goal over the next five years is to be happy." Be specific.

_____

_____

_____

_____

_____

_____

_____

_____

"It must be borne in mind that the tragedy of life doesn't lie in not reaching your goal. The tragedy lies in having no goal to reach. It isn't a calamity to die with dreams unfulfilled, but it is a calamity not to dream. It is not a disaster to be unable to capture your ideal, but it is a disaster to have no ideal to capture. It is not a disgrace not to reach the stars, but it is a disgrace to have no stars to reach for. Not failure, but low aim is sin."
- Benjamin E Mays

BIG!

DREAM BIG!

"Most people don't aim too high and miss. They aim too low and hit. — Bob Mouawad

"So many of our dreams at first seem impossible, then seem improbable, and then, when we summon the will, they soon see inevitable. "

—Christopher Reeve

There isn't one person in ten thousand who can write down his or her most exciting dreams without thinking "it's probably impossible."
The truth is, virtually anything is possible - nothing is too good to be true.

TRADING A PAPER CLIP FOR A HOUSE:

Thinking big, Kyle MacDonald started small—with a paperclip to be exact. He posted in on Craigslist as a barter and got a fish-shaped pen for it. he then traded the pen for something better. One trade led to another and another, until MacDonald finally found himself the new owner of a three-bedroom house.

Either you are living out someone else's dream for you, or you are designing your own life.

What would you attempt if you knew you could not fail? Write down a dream that you would love to pursue if you absolutely knew you could attain it. (It may be more doable than you think.)

_____

_____

_____

_____

_____

_____

_____

_____

_____

_____

EXPLORE THE WORLD AND DISCOVER PLACES IN YOU.

Life is truly a ride. We're all strapped in and no one can stop it. When the doctor slaps your behind, he's ripping your ticket and away you go. As you make each passage from youth to adulthood to maturity, sometimes you put your arms up and scream, sometimes you just hang onto that bar in front of you. But the ride is the thing. I think the most you can hope for at the end of life is that your hair is messed, you're out of breath and you didn't throw up. — Unknown

TAKE YOURSELF BY SURPRISE

Be unlike you now and then. Escape the treadmill of predictability. Wear colored socks. Take the scenic route to work. Re-tune your radio to Beethoven or Mariachi musick for awhile. Feed the birds at lunch. Give blood or visit the food bank. Call your mother. Plant a flaming yellow rhododendron. Buy a vegetable or fruit you've never tried before. Write a love letter to your significant other. Turn off the TV and talk to your kids.

Strike out in some new directions. Learn martial arts or creative dance. make a spectacular presentation. Obliterate your sales goal. Dream a wonderful dream. prepare an astounding meal. Tell an outrageous joke. Savor life. Remember, we only pass this way once.

_____

_____

_____

_____

_____

_____

_____

_____

MOUNT EVEREST

NORTHERN LIGHTS

THE GRAND CANYON

THE NILE

MOUNT KILIMANJARO

THE AMAZON RIVER

MOJAVE DESERT

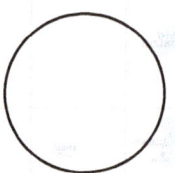

_____

YELLOWSTONE NATIONAL PARK

THE EIFFEL TOWER

NIAGARA FALLS

_____

THE GREAT BARRIER REEF

YOSEMITE NATIONAL PARK

EMPIRE STATE BUILDING

_____

LIVE AN ADVENTURE

This is the only life you get! What will be your adventure?
Check the boxes of your top your top destinations or make your own list, but go see
them for yourself!

_____   _____

_____   _____

_____   _____

_____   _____

_____   _____

_____   _____

_____   _____

_____   _____

"Because of our routines we forget that life is an
ongoing adventure." —Maya Angelou

WHERE DO YOU COME FROM?

TAP YOUR ROOTS | MEET YOUR ANCESTORS | SEE YOUR HOMELAND

Who are your ancestors?
Where did it all start?

Whoever they were, make your next vacation a trip to your homeland, go see where you came from. Walk the streets, explore the villages where they were born. Get a taste of their dreams, hopes and aspirations. Try to eat where they ate; sleep where the slept; pray where they prayed. You have a special role in a long line family members.

You deserve it! Go see, hear, feel, taste and touch your roots for yourself.

If you don't know where to start, simple go online and search for ancestry, you'll find your family tree and lineage. You'll learn fascinating things about those responsible for bringing you into the world. Their occupations, their struggles, their journeys will never cease to amaze you.

Write your ancestral story:

_____

_____

_____

_____

_____

_____

_____

_____

YOU ARE A CRAZY GENIUS

In 2005 three college guys wanted to share videos online with their friends. So they piece-mealed together an easy way for others to have the experience—and started their own little company called YouTube. Only 1 year later they sold that tiny company to Google for $1.6 billion and were named "Invention of the Year" by "Time" magazine.

What is your Youtube? The world needs your crazy genius. One crazy idea can transform the world.

WHAT'S YOUR CRAZY GENIUS?

_____

_____

_____

_____

_____

_____

_____

> *"Thousands of perceptions, hunches, ideas and intuitions race through our brains every day. Some are pure genius. Give them the red light for at least long enough to write them down." — Ralph Ford*

WHY NOT YOU?
WHY NOT NOW?

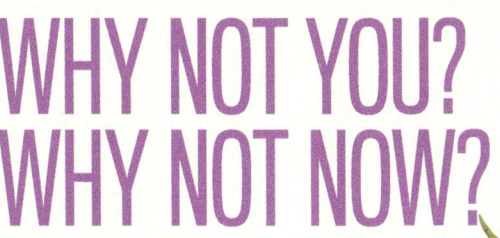

Most people spend all their lives on a boring little island called the "Someday Island." Someday I'll run with the bulls. Someday I'll hike the Himalayas. Someday I'll have an adventure. Someday I'll be happy. LIfe is not a dress rehearsal. Life is here and it is now. Reach out and seize it, you deserve it!

List five things you've been procrastinating about the plan to take at least a little bit of action on all five this week. Do it now!

So, who are you
REALLY?

Seattle is a beautiful place, but in the 1980s I was living in a beat-up beach cabin. I had an old TV, a lumpy futon, and one of those white plastic Princess phones. I was basically broke, but my noisy old refrigerator was stuffed with fresh vegetables, eggs, fruit, beer and frozen pizza— and I had a spectacular view of Puget Sound, the Olympic Mountains and the Seattle skyline.

That year, I volunteered to host a college exchange student from Guinea-Bissau, Africa. When I picked him up at the airport, Salvatore was way to spot. He was 23, tall and regal-looking, with a huge smile and lustrous blue-black skin. He had lived his entire as a barefoot fisherman in a small native village located on a big river deep in the jungle of Guinea-Bissau— and now his village had raised the money to send him to study U.S. Fisheries on their behalf. He had travelled directly fro his African village to Seattle, and I could see he was astonished at what he saw as we drove through the beautiful city.

When we arrived at my raggedy cabin I was worried that Salvatore might be disappointed with his new accommodations. He seemed somber as I showed him the little bedroom, bathroom, kitchen, TV and telephone. What was Salvatore thinking? I decided to take him out on the little deck to try to impress him with the view. The snow-clad mountains were spread out against the sky that day, and one of Seattle's majestic white ferries was gliding across the sparkling waters of Puget Sound. We stood there silently for awhile, and then Salvatore turned to me with his brow deeply knit in thought.

"You are king?" He asked. "No," I laughed, "I'm just an everyday person like you." Salvatore was silent for a moment, and he turned again and said quite clearly and emphatically, "you are a king." And it suddenly dawned on me that he was right. All these years I had been a king and not known it. -Scott Sabol, Ph.D.

If you have food in your refrigerator, clothes on your back, a roof overhead and a place to sleep…you are richer than 75% of the world's population.

If you have a little money in the bank or spare change in a dish someplace…you are among the top 8% of the world's wealthy.

If you can drink from your kitchen faucet whenever you want…you are more fortunate by far than 1.5 billion people who have no access to clean water at all.

If you can attend a church or a political rally without fear of harassment, arrest, torture or death…you have the kind of freedom denied to more than three billion people in the world.

If you can read this message, you are more blessed that two billion people who cannot read at all.

If your everyday problems are weighing you down, there are millions of people on earth who would gladly trade places with you right now—problems and all—and feel they have been royally blessed.

- Remember: "From those to whom much is given, much is expected."

YOU ARE ROYALTY

You were not born to "GO" through life, but rather to "GROW" through life.

Realize that the journey of life is not about being right or pretending that you know it all—it's about learning and growing every step of the way. Make your life an adventure. Decide TODAY that your commitment to learning and growing over the next five years is bigger than your commitment to staying the same.

I would rather be asjes than dust; I would rather that my spark should burn out in a brilliant blaze than it should be stifled by dry-rot; I would rather be in superb meteor, every atom of me in a magnificent glow than in a sleepy and permanent planet; the proper function of man is to live, not to exist; I shall not waste my days in trying to prolong them; I shall USE my time.

- Jack London

MASTER A SKILL: Don't just be good, be great, take an "interest" and elevate it into an art form. Learn to do something so well that people will com from miles around just to watch you do it again and again. Become a Master.

KICK A HABIT: If there is anything in your life that is holding you back, now is the time to think about changing it. What habits are currently preventing the best that is in you? (on average, it takes about 30 days to change a negative habit into a positive habit—but the benefits will last a lifetime!)

TRANSFORM NEGATIVES: What bugs you? A fast track to happiness and fulfillment is to zero in on whatever make you unhappy, and turn those negatives into positives. Identifying what bugs you about yourself or your life is a lesson in instant clarity.

GET FIT: Yoga, running, rock climing, hula hoop—it doesn't matter what you do, but do it. Get in the best shape of your life. Over the next five years you can have the body, the energy and the health you've always wanted.

life is now...

It's never too late or too early. Right now is a good time.

> *"Here is the test to determine whether your mission on earth is finished: if you're alive, it isn't."* – *Richard Bach*

AT AGE 7   Mozart wrote his first symphony.

AT 14   Country singer LeAnn Rimes won her first two Grammy Awards.

AT 16   Swimmer Shane Gould won three Olympic Gold Medals.

AT 17   Joan of Arc led an Army in defense of France

AT 20   Debbi Fields founded Mrs. Fields cookie company

AT 21   Fred DeLuca co-founded Subway with just $1,000 in the bank

AT 43   John F kennedy ran for the US Presidency and won

AT 45   Boxer George Foreman regained the heavyweight championship of the world

AT 46   Jack Nicklaus won his sixth Masters tournament

AT 54   Jockey Willie Shoemaker won the Kentucky Derby

AT 57   Ray Kroc founded MacDonald's

AT 62   Colonel Sanders devoted himself to Kentucky Fried Chicken

AT 78   Grandma Moses started painting and was still participating in one-woman art shows well into her nineties

AT 83   Architect Frank Lloyd Wright was asked which of his masterpieces was the best. "My next one," he said.

AT 84   Titian painted his famous "Allegory of the Battle of Lepanto."

AT 86   Ruth Rothfarb ran the Boston Marathon in just over five hours. "You lose a lot of speed between 80 and 86," she joked

ON HIS 104TH BIRTHDAY   Cal Evans was interviewed by a Denver reporter. "have you lived in Denver all your life?" asked the reporter. Cal laughed and replied, "not yet, Sonny."

Whether you're five or 105, you have a lifetime ahead of you-so renew your dreams!
What are you passionate about? What is something you've always wanted to do but haven't done? Right now is a good time.

Make a difference. You are the one you've been waiting for.

Write down your ideas and go make the world better

You don't have to quit your job or sacrifice your family or all your free time to make a difference in the world. One person like you can change the social landscape of our country in a few hours a week.

How?

"If every American donated five hours a week." writes Whoopi Goldberg. "it would equal the labor of twenty million full time volunteers."

May God bless you with tears to shed for those who suffer from pain, rejection, starvation and war, so that you will reach out your hand to comfort them and change their pain into joy. And may God bless you with the foolishness to think that you can make a difference in the world, so that you will do the things with others tell you cannot be done.
—A Franciscan Benediction

What do you care about? If you think somebody should do something about it, be somebody. Make a list of causes you are passionate about, then get involved.

_____

_____

_____

_____

_____

_____

"One of my best moves is to surround myself with friends who, instead of asking, "Why?" are quick to say, "Why not?" that attitude is contagious."
Oprah Winfrey

FRIENDS

Surround yourself with people who believe you can. By all means, share your goals—but only share them with people who can help you attain them.

Benchmark test for choosing friends: Will spending time with this person drag me down or lift me up? Will he or she make me want to be a better person? A happier person? A more successful person? Will he or she help me achieve my most important goals? If not, find some friends who will.

LIST FIVE PEOPLE WHO CAN HELP YOU ACHIEVE YOUR DREAMS AND GOALS.

....

....

....

....

....

FINISH
STRONG

An elderly man, in the final days of his life, is lying in bed alone. He awakens to see a late group of people clustered around his bed. Their faces are loving, but sad. Confused, the old man smiles weakly and whispers, "You must be my childhood friends come to say boos-bye. I am so grateful" moving closer, the tallest figure gently grasps the old man's hand and replies, "Yes, we are you best and oldest friends, but long ago you abandoned us. For we are the unfulfilled promises of your youth. We are the unrealized hopes, dreams and plans that you once felt deeply in your heart, but never pursued. We are the unique talents that you never refine. The special gifts that you never discovered. Old friend, we have not come to comfort you, but to die with you." - From "I Believe in You"

When you reach the end of your life do you want to be one of the people who are glad they did, or one of the people who wish they had?

Start doing the things today that will matter tomorrow. Don't leave this world without giving it your all. The best inheritance you can leave your kids is and example of how to live a full and meaningful life.

"This is a record of you time. This is your movie. Live out your dreams and fantasies. Whisper question to the sphinx at night. Sit for hours at sidewalk cafes and drink with your heroes. Believe in the unknown **For it is there.** Live with flowers and music and books and paintings and sculpture. Keep a record of your time. Learn to read well. Learn to listen and speak well. Know your country, know your world, know your history, know yourself. Take care of yourself physically and mentally. You owe it to your self. Be good to those around you and do all things with passion. Give all that you can. Remember, life is short and death is long."

— Fritz Shoulder

You will never have more time than you do right now.

Close your eyes for a few minutes and imagine that today is you 100th birthday. Your children and grandchildren are throwing a party-and a newspaper reporter has come to interview you.

What do you want to tel the reporter about your life? Your accomplishments? Your regrets? Now, Open your eyes. It's not too late—you have a fresh start on life!

_____

_____

_____

_____

_____

Share This Experience with Someone!

Change you. Change the world.

A great life would naturally bring more meaning, purpose, love, laughter, wonder and adventure to your days. And, at the end of your journey you would look back on a life of significance, rather than regret—knowing in your heart that you left the world better than you found it. Knowing that you made a difference in the lives of others. Knowing that you got something wonderful out of it, and you gave something wonderful back.

A great life, of course, is not something we experience, it's something we create. **That's what this book is all about.**

Our mission is to empower ordinary people to make extraordinary change in themselves and in the world. We are all well aware of the horrific global facts, statistics and stories that cause us to want to change the world. From Politics to racism, drug addiction, deadly diseases, rape, murder, abuse, government, poverty, sex trafficking, prostitution, layoffs, riots, and all that I missed...

Most of us want **CHANGE**

We want to change the economy, change the government, change our health, change our habits, change our world. We all want a better life. We even post, tweet, and pin cool quotes, pics, and videos in an attempt to inspire us and those around us. But the statistics continue to rise; our debt increases, our weight goes up, our relationships are strained, our life is no better this year than last.

Let's empower ordinary people to make extraordinary change in the world.

So, what's the answer?
What's the solution?
How do WE change the world?

The answer, the solution is **YOU. YOU CHANGE**. In order to Change **THE** World, you first have to Change **YOUR** world.

To make the world a healthier place to live, you have to become healthy. To lower the divorce rate, you have to improve your marriage. To change the economy, you have to change your economy and earn more, become more valuable to the market place.

YOU are not here by mistake. (no matter what you're older sibling told you)
The world needs the best you got, the best you, in every aspect; financially, healthy, socially, spiritually, educationally, and family. Starting today and for years to come use this book to **CHANGE YOU — CHANGE THE WORLD.** Transform is more than merely a book, it's a living, breathing organism, it's a movement, it's your life.

This is **YOUR** time. You have important discoveries to make. You have important talents to develop. You have important gifts to give the world. *You don't have to take life the way it comes. You are the artist. You get to design the life you want to live and the way you want it to be.*

"Don't say you don't have enough time. You have exactly the same number of hours per day that were given to Helen Keller, Louis Pasteur, Michaelangelo, Mother Tersa, Leonardo da Vinci, Thomas Jefferson and Albert Einstein."

- H. Jackson Brown Jr.

DECIDE what YOU want in YOUR life and what STRATEGY will you use to get it.

This is your life, and you only get one life, so you don't have time to mess around and miss one second of it. So, what is it going to be? You decide. Right here. Right now. Starting this moment, you can make your life the most exciting, fulfilling, productive and magnificent years of life so far - or you can give in fear, doubt, and bury your dreams in a hole.

The purpose of this book is to get you to discover your one and only, true, real you and your sole purpose in life. To inspire you to reach within and live your dreams. The goal is not to provide you with a list of "to do's", but rather a look inside your heart and soul that stirs your genius to become all you're meant to be, all you were created to be. To find the seamless and universal power inside you that is able to do exceedingly, abundantly, beyond all that you can ask, think, or imagine.

In the following pages you'll find fresh ways of thinking about different areas of your life.

It's Your Life. **What do you really want to do with it? What do you really want to have? Where do you want to go? Who do you want to help? What do you want to learn? Who do you want to become?**

Here's a good way to think about it; If you only had 5 years left on earth, that'd be 260 weeks, and 1820 days. What would you do with it? What's possible?

- In Just 3 years after being fired from their home-improvement jobs, Arthur Blank and Bernie Marcus launched Home Depot to over $1 Billion in sales.

- From the age of 30 to 35 Jeff Bezos, Founder of Amazon went from living in a 500 square foot apartment to have a net worth of over $10 Billion. In just 5 years.

- In less than 5 years Shakespeare wrote; "Hamlet, Othello, King Lear and Macbeth" as well as 5 other famous plays.

- In just 5 years Columbus discovered the Bahamas, Cuba, Hispaniola, North and South America.